Checkmate!
The Game of Chess

Applying Strategies from Simple to Complex Problems

Greg Roza

PowerMath™

The Rosen Publishing Group's
PowerKids Press™
New York

Published in 2004 by The Rosen Publishing Group, Inc.
29 East 21st Street, New York, NY 10010

Copyright © 2004 by The Rosen Publishing Group, Inc.

Book Design: Ron A. Churley

Photo Credits: Cover and all interior illustrations by Ron A. Churley; p. 5 © Archivo Iconografico/Corbis;
p. 9 © Jose Luis Pelaez, Inc./Corbis; p. 30 © Ronnie Kaufman/Corbis.

Library of Congress Cataloging-in-Publication Data

Roza, Greg.
  Checkmate! The game of chess : applying strategies from simple to
complex problems / Greg Roza.
       p. cm. — (PowerMath)
Includes index.
Summary: Introduces the game of chess and its basic moves, then shows
how to apply problem-solving skills to chess problems of varying
difficulty.
  ISBN 0-8239-8996-8 (lib. bdg.)
  ISBN 0-8239-8925-9 (pbk.)
  6-Pack ISBN 0-8239-7453-7
  1. Chess—Juvenile literature. [1. Chess.] I. Title. II. Series.
  GV1446 .R69 2004
  794.1—dc21
                              2002156337

Manufactured in the United States of America

Contents

The History of Chess

Chess is a very old game that involves two "armies." Each game is a heated "battle" fought by foot soldiers, brave knights, kings, and queens. Chess does not deal with numbers and equations, but it is like math in many ways. Playing chess has always involved problem-solving skills, which are important when working out math problems that have many steps.

Most historians agree that chess was invented in the early 500s, but some think it may have been invented earlier. Many believe it appeared first in India, but others believe it was invented in China or in Persia, which today is called Iran. Through the years, many countries created their own **versions** of the game of chess.

Between 600 A.D. and 1200 A.D., chess spread to Europe, where it became very popular. By the late 1400s, chess had developed into the game we know today.

This book from the early 1300s shows a ruler named Otto IV playing chess with a woman. Otto IV ruled part of what is now Germany.

Beginning the Game

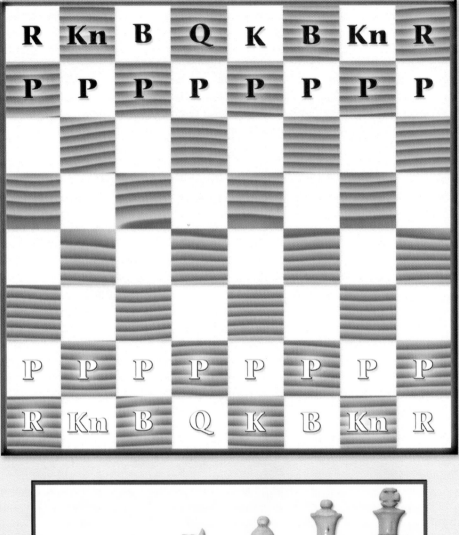

R	Kn	B	Q	K	B	Kn	R
P	P	P	P	P	P	P	P
P	P	P	P	P	P	P	P
R	Kn	B	Q	K	B	Kn	R

pawn   rook   knight   bishop   queen   king

P   **R**   **Kn**   **B**   **Q**   **K**

Let's Play Chess!

Chess is played by 2 people on a game board made up of 64 squares set up in 8 **rows** of 8 squares each. Each player starts off with 16 pieces—or men—set up in 2 rows. There are 6 different types of men, and each moves in a different way. One player has white pieces and the other player has black ones. The player with the white men makes the first move.

You take a man from your **opponent** by moving 1 of your men onto the same square that their man is on. A piece is "in check" if your opponent can take it from you in 1 more move. The goal of chess is to **capture** your opponent's king while stopping them from capturing your king.

It is important to think ahead when playing chess. A move that seems like a good one may turn out to be a bad move depending on what your opponent does next. Sometimes it's a good idea to let your opponent take 1 of your pieces if it means that you can make a strong move on your next turn.

When a player's king is in check, they must move it out of check. A player is not allowed to make any move with their king that would put the king in check. The winner of a game is the player who can put their opponent's king in check and leave them no way to get out of it. This is called **checkmate**.

When neither player has enough pieces left to put their opponent's king in checkmate, the game ends in a draw, or tie. When a player's king is not in check, but any move they make will put their king into check, the game ends in a type of draw that is known as a **stalemate**. A player who is winning must think ahead to avoid causing a stalemate when they could have won instead.

A draw is sometimes considered as good as a win, especially if a player who does not have much experience can force a more experienced player into a draw.

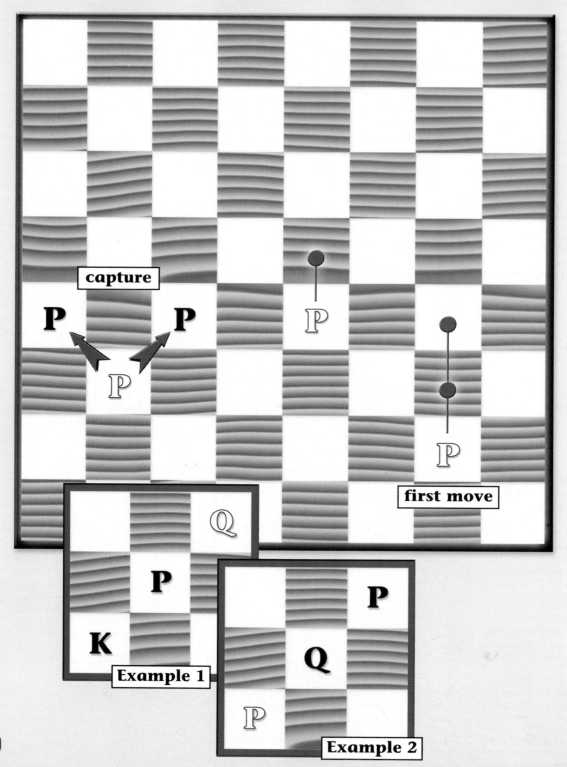

capture

first move

Example 1

Example 2

Chessmen

Pawns

Each player starts the game with 8 pieces called pawns lined up in the second row. Pawns are the foot soldiers in chess. They move forward 1 space at a time. If the pawn has not yet moved from its starting square and there are no other men in its way, it may move forward 2 spaces. Pawns can only capture other pieces by moving **diagonally** forward 1 space.

Pawns are the weakest men on the board. They move slowly and are often trapped or captured by other pieces. Pawns are most useful when they protect more important pieces from being captured. A pawn that makes it to an opponent's back row is **promoted** to another type of piece, usually a queen, since she is the most powerful piece on the board.

pawn

In the first example, the black pawn protects its king by standing between the king and the white queen. In the second example, the black pawn will capture the white pawn if the white pawn takes the black queen. The player who controls the white pieces will probably be willing to give up their weak pawn to capture the powerful black queen.

Knights

Each player starts the game with 2 knights. These pieces often look like horses. The knights begin in the back row, in the second space from the outer edges of the chessboard.

The knight moves in an L-shape. First, the knight moves 2 spaces in the row or **column** in which he is positioned, and then he moves 1 space to the left or right. The knight is a very useful piece in the beginning of the game because it is the only man that can leap over other men. The knight cannot land on a square occupied by a man of the same color, but it can move quickly around a crowded board to attack a man of the opposite color. Knights can be very powerful pieces when used together or when used with other pieces.

knight

In the example at the bottom of page 13, the black knight has both the white king and white queen in check. This move is called a "fork." White must move their king out of check, which means the black knight can capture the white queen on its next move.

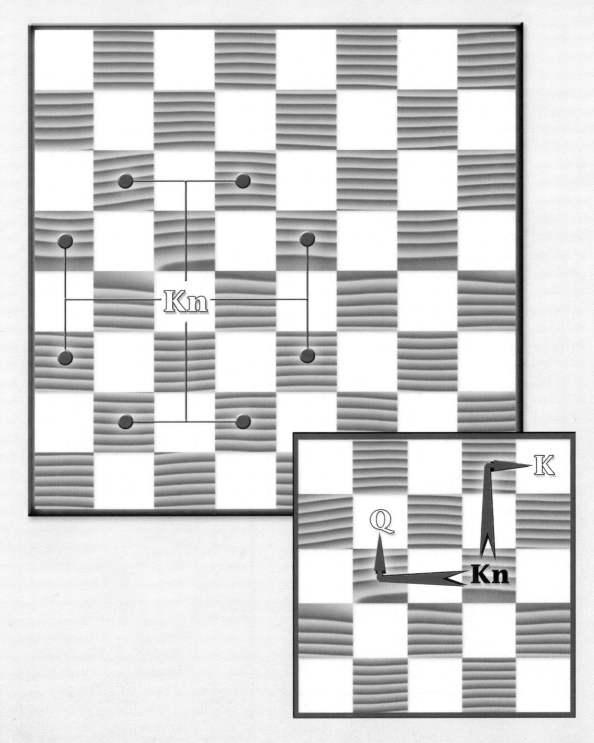

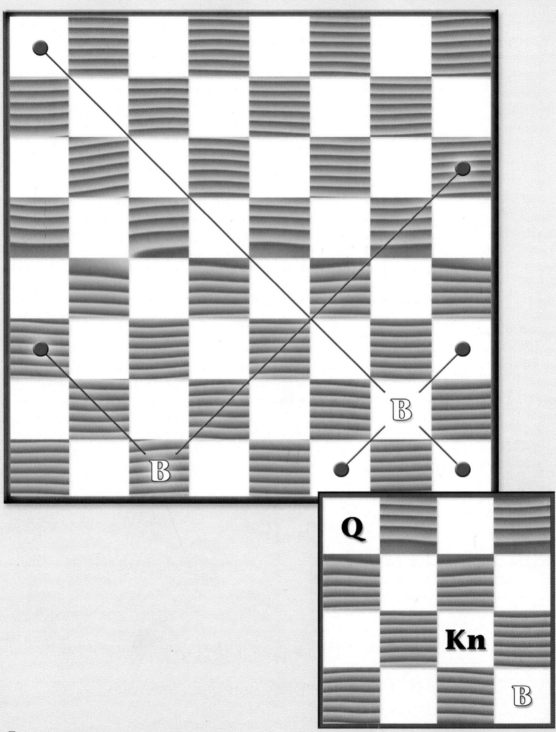

Bishops

Each player begins the game with 2 bishops in the back row, in the third space from the outer edges of the chessboard. One of the bishops moves only on white spaces. The other bishop moves only on black spaces. Bishops move diagonally. As long as there are no other pieces in its way, a bishop can attack a piece that is all the way across the board. They can also **retreat** quickly if they need to come back to their side of the board to protect the king.

Since 1 bishop moves only on white spaces and the other moves only on black ones, they are powerful pieces when they are used together. They can cover a wider area than either could when used alone.

bishop

In the example at the bottom of page 14, the white bishop has made a move called a "pin." The black knight can't move because that will put a more powerful piece, the black queen, in check. The white bishop has "pinned" the black knight to the black queen.

Rooks

Each player starts the game with 2 rooks, which often look like castles. The rooks are positioned on either end of the back row. They can move in a straight line forward, backward, left, or right, as long as there are no other pieces in their way.

It is difficult to move rooks during the early part of most games because there are too many pieces in the way. Many chess players prefer not to use the rooks during the first part of the game. This is partly because they are trapped behind other men, but also because they provide excellent **defense** for their king. A rook is one of the more powerful men on the chessboard. Two rooks alone, or a rook and another man, can also easily put the opponent's king in checkmate.

rook

The black rook in the example at the bottom of page 17 has made a move called a "skewer." The white king must move out of check. Moving the king will allow the black rook to take the white bishop.

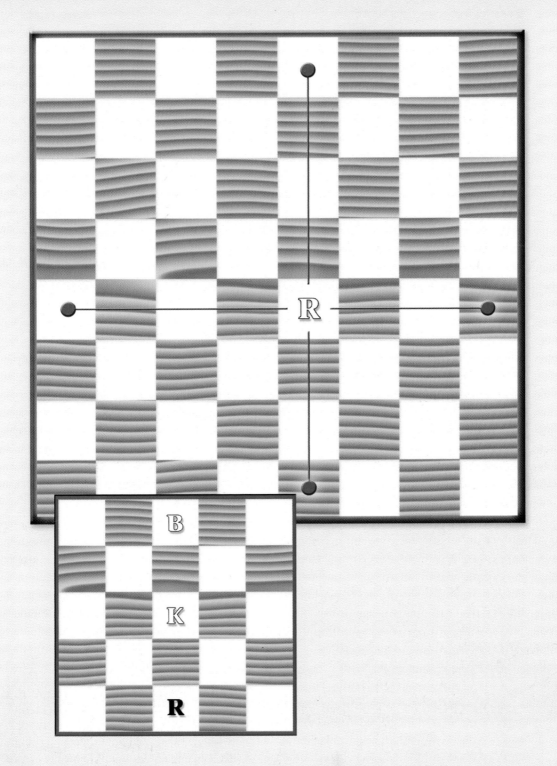

This diagram shows why the queen is such a powerful and valuable piece. The black player must move the black king out of check or move another black piece between the black king and the white queen. On their next turn, the white player will be able to capture a black piece and perhaps put the black king in check again!

Queens

Each player has 1 queen, which begins the game in the middle of the back row on the space of her own color. The queen can move straight or diagonally as long as there are no other pieces in her way. The queen can move quickly, she can guard several of her own men at the same time, and she can retreat quickly when she needs to.

The queen can move as soon as one of the pawns in front of her is moved, allowing a player to control the middle of the chessboard early in the game. However, your opponent can use less important men to chase the queen. If you must use your moves to keep your queen from being taken, you will not be able to move other men forward into attacking position.

queen

The king stands next to the queen in the back row. The king can only move 1 space in any direction, as long as that space is not occupied by another man of the same color, and as long as he is not putting himself in check.

There are 2 main goals in a game of chess: protect your king, and capture your opponent's king. Since the king moves slowly, it is important to protect him. Many players like to leave the king in the back row behind the pawns. With the king safe, a player is free to attack their opponent. Watch out, though. A good chess player will find ways to break through your defenses and put your king in danger.

king

Kings and rooks have a special defensive move called "castling" that helps protect the king. When there are no men between one of the rooks and the king, and neither of those pieces have moved yet, a player can move the king toward the rook 2 spaces, then jump the king with the rook. A king cannot move out of check by castling.

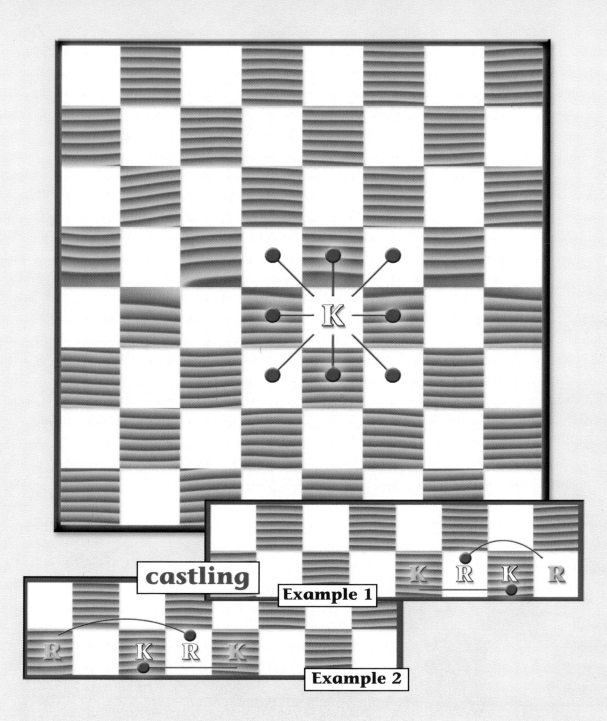

castling

Example 1

Example 2

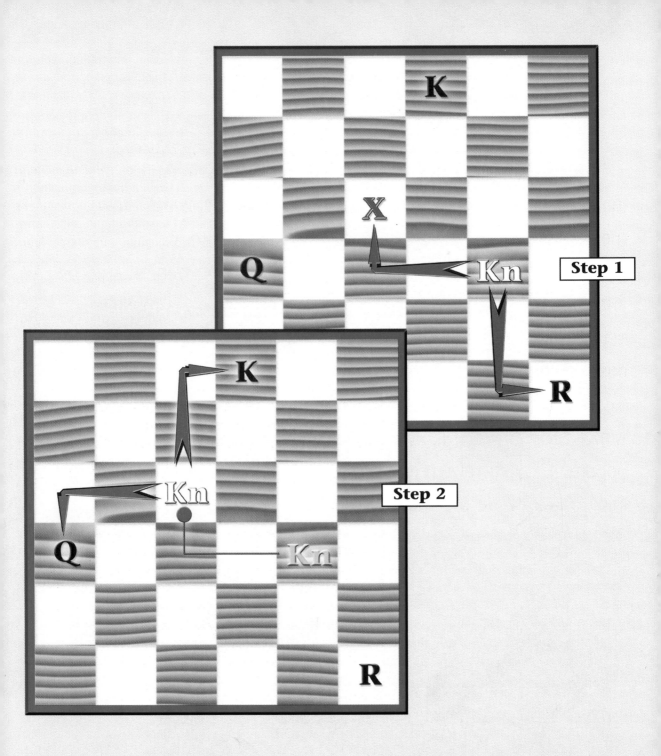

Step 1

Step 2

22

Plan Your Attack, but Watch Your Back!

Understanding how the chessmen move is just the first step in learning how to play chess. Chess is a game of **strategy**. This means that instead of just moving a man each turn, it is important to plan several turns ahead before making any move in order to be sure that your plan will work. A good strategy involves multiple steps. Sometimes it is a good idea to plan more than 1 strategy in case the first strategy fails.

While planning your attack, you must also plan your defense. A move might seem like a good move when you make it, but your opponent's next move might change that. This is why you need to think ahead when playing chess.

Here is a simple example of chess strategy. It is white's turn. The white knight could take the black rook, but is there a better move? Yes! By moving the white knight to the space marked with the X, white can put both the black king and black queen in check. Black must move the king out of check, which means the white knight will be able to take the black queen on their next turn!

The white player in this chess problem still has their queen. White has an advantage over the black player, who only has a bishop and a rook left. It is the black player's move. Is there a way for the black player to take the white queen in 2 moves?

The black player could put the white king in check by moving the black rook 1 space to the right. Is that a good move? No, because the white queen could take the black rook and put the black king in check. Is there a better move?

There is! Black can use their bishop to "pin" the white queen to the white king. Then the white player cannot move their queen out of check because that would put their king in check. Now that's a good strategy!

Even though the white queen could take the black bishop, the black player would respond by taking the white queen with their king or rook. Now the black player has the advantage!

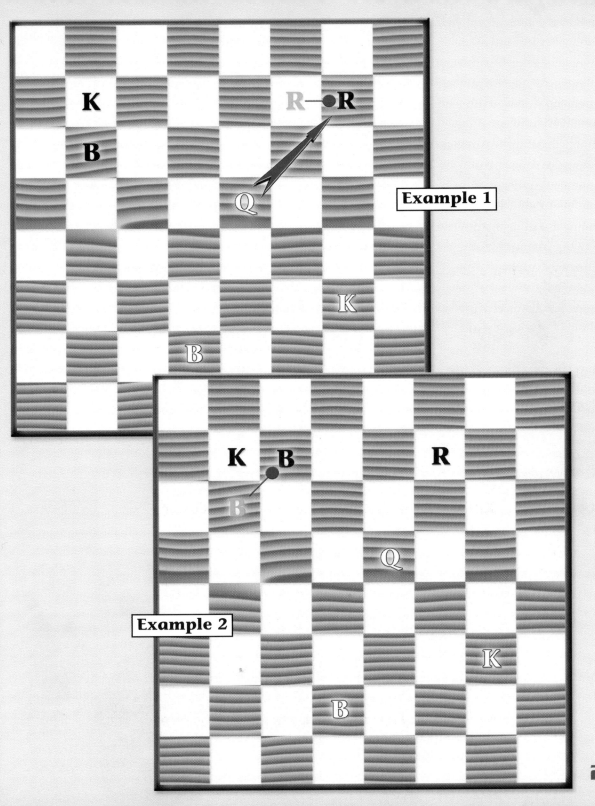

Example 1

Example 2

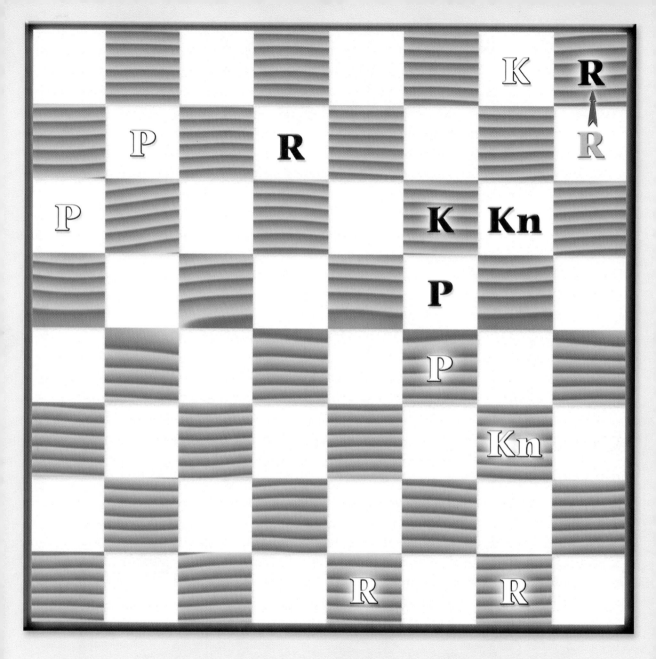

The End of the Game

Strong opening moves are important to winning a game of chess. However, you cannot win a game unless you can make strong ending moves, too. When there are very few men left on the board, winning a game can be tricky. You must plan ahead.

Study the chess game in this picture. Both players have lost their queens. White is very close to promoting a pawn, which means that they would regain their queen. This is a tempting move because white would surely have the stronger army. However, if white decides to promote the white pawn, then black can move one of their rooks into the last row where it will be protected by the black knight. Checkmate! The black player wins the game.

Before turning the page, study the original position. Could you win the game if you were the white player? Here's a hint: You may need to lose a few of your men to put your opponent's king in checkmate. Plan your strategy, and you can do it!

Let's go back to the way the board was set up on the previous page. Since black will be able to put white in checkmate on their next turn, white needs to put black in check to avoid losing the game.

Step 1

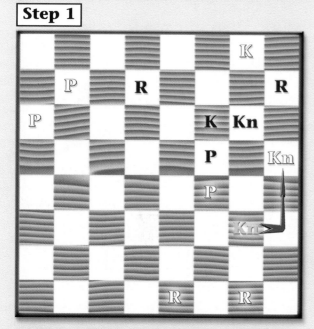

By thinking ahead, you will see that using the knight to put the black king in check is a good idea for two reasons. First, it stops the black rook from putting the white king in checkmate. Second, it clears the way for white's rook to join the fight.

Step 2

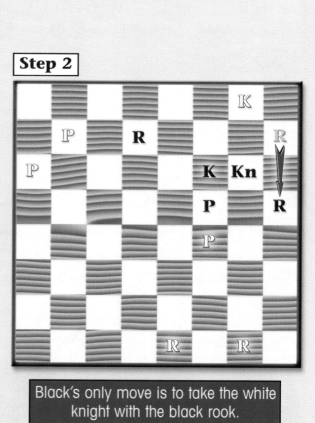

Black's only move is to take the white knight with the black rook.

Step 3

White then takes the black knight with the white rook and puts the black king in check at the same time.

Step 4

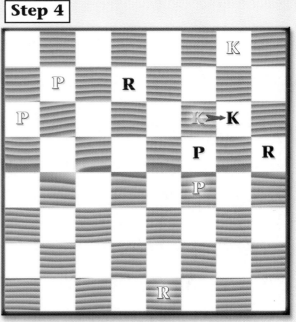

Black's only move is to take the white rook with the black king

Step 5

White moves their other rook up. Checkmate! The game is over.

Exercise Your Brain

The basic rules of chess are simple to learn. Each chessman moves in a specific way, and that is all you really need to know to start playing. However, some people spend years—sometimes their whole lives—mastering the game of chess. Chess players improve their playing style with every game. Chess is exercise for your brain!

Chess teaches you to solve problems that have multiple steps, and it teaches you the importance of strategy. These skills will help you improve your math skills, too. Some math problems are simple, like $2 + 2 = 4$. Other math problems require more than simple addition or subtraction. Some math problems require a good strategy, just like the game of chess.

Glossary

capture (KAP-chur) To move one of your chessmen to a square occupied by a chessman of the opposite color and remove that man from the board.

checkmate (CHEK-mayt) The end of a game of chess, which happens when a player cannot move their king out of check.

column (KAH-luhm) A line of squares on a chessboard that extends from one player's side to the other player's side.

defense (dih-FENS) Anything that guards something else and keeps it safe.

diagonal (dy-A-guh-nuhl) A straight line that cuts across a space at an angle.

opponent (uh-POH-nuhnt) The person or team against whom you play in a game.

promote (pruh-MOHT) To raise something to a higher level of importance.

retreat (rih-TREET) To move back.

row (ROH) A line of squares that extends from left to right on a chessboard.

stalemate (STAYL-mayt) A draw in a game of chess that happens when a player's king is not in check, but any move the player makes puts their king in check.

strategy (STRA-tuh-jee) Thoughtful and skillful planning.

version (VUHR-zhun) A different form of something.

Index